Off We Go!

by Joanna Lake

OXFORD
UNIVERSITY PRESS

We will visit
Beth and Raf.

We go in the van. It is red.

We will go
to the shops.

Nan pulls the bag. She is quick.

We go to fish. It is lots of fun.

This rod belongs to me!

We rush to the buses.

We sing a long song.

We run and run. We dash to the finish.

I think I can win it!

I get a hat. I get a bucket.

We fill up the bag.

Thanks!
I will push it!

Off we go! We will relax.

Look Back

Encourage students to use the images to review the topic.